New Mexico
The Land of Enchantment

Miriam Coleman

PowerKiDS press™
New York

Published in 2011 by The Rosen Publishing Group, Inc.
29 East 21st Street, New York, NY 10010

First Edition

Editor: Joanne Randolph
Book Design: Greg Tucker
Layout Design: Kate Laczynski
Photo Researcher: Jessica Gerweck

Library of Congress Cataloging-in-Publication Data

Coleman, Miriam.
  New Mexico : Land of Enchantment / Miriam Coleman. — 1st ed.
      p. cm. — (Our amazing states)
  Includes index.
  ISBN 978-1-4488-0658-4 (library binding) — ISBN 978-1-4488-0748-2 (pbk.) —
ISBN 978-1-4488-0749-9 (6-pack)
  1. New Mexico—Juvenile literature. I. Title.
  F796.3.C65 2011
  978.9—dc22
                                                2010000239

Manufactured in the United States of America

CPSIA Compliance Information: Batch #WS10PK: For Further Information contact Rosen Publishing, New York, New York at 1-800-237-9932

Contents

The Land of Enchantment

New Mexico is in the southwestern United States. It is one of the four-corner states, along with Utah, Colorado, and Arizona. These four states get this name because one of their corners meets at a point with the other three states. New Mexico's lively **culture** comes from the mix of Spanish, Mexican, Native American, cowboy, and U.S. settlers who have made this place their home over the years. Many people in New Mexico speak Spanish.

New Mexico's landscape is a mix of high, rocky mountains, white sand dunes, and desert valleys. Red stone arches stand out against the blue desert sky and hot springs bubble out of the ground. It is no wonder New Mexico is nicknamed the Land of **Enchantment**!

Many people come to see New Mexico's Carlsbad Caverns. *Inset*: Here a mother and her son enjoy the view from the Sandia Mountains, east of Albuquerque, New Mexico.

From Old Mexico to New Mexico

For thousands of years, New Mexico has been home to Native American peoples. These include the Mogollons, Anasazis, Pueblos, Navajos, Apaches, and Comanches. Spanish explorers, such as Francisco Vásquez de Coronado, came through New Mexico in the early 1500s looking for gold. Spain set up a colony in New Mexico in 1598. In 1609, Sante Fe was founded as the colony's capital.

In 1821, New Mexico became part of Mexico when Mexico freed itself from Spanish rule. In 1846, the United States fought Mexico over the land in the Mexican War. At the war's end in 1848, New Mexico became a U.S. territory. In 1912, New Mexico became the forty-seventh state.

The Battle of Buena Vista took place on February 23, 1847, during the Mexican War. In this battle, 5,000 U.S. troops fought off 20,000 Mexican soldiers.

Chaco Canyon

In northwestern New Mexico, there is a canyon that is 15 miles (24 km) long, with sandstone walls 300 feet (91 m) high. Within these canyon walls lie the **ruins** of a **civilization** that **thrived** in New Mexico between AD 950 and 1150. The people who lived there were **ancestors** of the Pueblo Indians. They made beautiful pottery, grew rich farms, and built roads. They also built giant houses called pueblos. They used great skill and planning to build these huge pueblos.

The area where these people lived is now called Chaco Culture National Historical Park. If you visit today, you can see the remains of buildings like Pueblo Bonita, which once held 800 rooms!

Here you can see some of the ruins at Chaco Canyon. Seeing the ruins and going to the Chaco Museum can help you learn about our country's past.

An Enchanted Landscape

New Mexico is the fifth-largest state, and it has a lot of different kinds of land. In the east, the Great Plains have high, flat grasslands. The Basin and Range Region has low, bowl-shaped deserts between mountain ranges. The Colorado Plateau is a mix of plains, canyons, cliffs, and mesas, which are hills with flat tops. New Mexico's highest point is part of the Rocky Mountains. Wheeler Peak is 13,167 feet (4,013 m) tall.

The Rio Grande is a river that flows through the middle of New Mexico. Elephant Butte Reservoir, which was formed by a dam on the Rio Grande, is New Mexico's largest lake. The Gila, San Juan, and Pecos rivers are also important in the state's landscape. New Mexico's **climate** is dry and warm.

These rocks are called the Cracked Eggs. They are found in New Mexico's Bisti Wilderness, which is full of oddly shaped and colorful rocks.

Wild New Mexico

You might think of deserts as places where nothing grows, but New Mexico's deserts are alive with cacti, mesquite, and purple and white sage. New Mexico's state flower is the yucca. The plant's small white flowers grow in groups among its thick, pointy green leaves. It grows well in New Mexico's hot, dry weather. Juniper trees, aspens, ponderosa pines, and scrub oaks also grow in the state.

New Mexico's state animal is the American black bear. Coyotes, mountain lions, elks, bobcats, and prairie dogs also make homes in the state. New Mexico's state bird is the greater roadrunner. This bird can run up to 15 miles per hour (24 km/h)!

Here a black bear cub rests on a log. The black bear became New Mexico's state animal in 1963.

At Work in New Mexico

Science is big business in New Mexico. **Research laboratories** like Los Alamos and Sandia National Laboratories offer jobs studying and making **nuclear** power and **weapons**. New Mexico also makes computers and **electronic equipment**. Energy products, such as coal, oil, natural gas, and uranium, are mined in the state, too.

New Mexico's ranches raise cattle for beef and milk. Its top crop is hay, which is generally used to feed cattle. New Mexico also grows a lot of chili peppers and pecans. Tourism is very important to the state. Many businesses count on people who come to the state to visit.

Tourism is an important business in New Mexico. Many people who travel there enjoy learning about the Native American culture in the state. *Inset*: Many tourists come to see Taos Pueblo.

Welcome to Santa Fe!

The capital of New Mexico is Santa Fe. Colonists from Spain founded the city in 1610. This makes Santa Fe the oldest capital in the United States! The oldest government building in the country is also in Santa Fe. The Palace of the Governors was built in 1610 and served as the home of 60 different governors from Spain, Mexico, and the United States. It is now a museum where you can learn about the settlement of New Mexico.

New Mexico has always drawn, or attracted, artists, who come to paint or sculpt in the peaceful desert setting. One of the artists known for painting in this state is Georgia O'Keeffe. You can see this rich artistic history at Santa Fe's New Mexico Museum of Art.

The New Mexico capitol, in Santa Fe, is called the Roundhouse. It does not look like other U.S. state capitols. It is the only round capitol in the country!

The Very Large Array

On New Mexico's Plains of San Agustin, 27 giant antennae reach up to the sky. The antennae are set in circular dishes that are 82 feet (25 m) across. Together these antennae form a huge **telescope**. The telescope is called the Very Large Array. It is used to study radio waves sent by stars trillions of miles (km) away.

The Very Large Array was built for the National Radio **Astronomy Observatory** in 1981. Scientists chose this place because it is far from any large cities or towns. There is not a lot of electrical activity on these plains that might get in the way of reading the radio waves. This is important to the scientists who are trying to gather facts about our universe.

These large dish shapes are some of the antennae in the Very Large Array. They can move to catch sound from different parts of space.

Visiting the Land of Enchantment

New Mexico is a place of natural wonders. It is home to Carlsbad Caverns, a group of caves that includes one of the world's largest rock chambers. Many people come to New Mexico to enjoy the outdoors. You can go rafting on the Rio Grande or skiing at Taos Ski Valley.

New Mexico holds a lot of history within its borders, but it is also bursting with living culture. In cities and villages, you can see Spanish and Native American dances and crafts. You can visit a Navajo reservation. There are plenty of museums where you can see art, pieces of history, or fossils, which are the remains of plants and animals that died a long time ago. If you are brave, you can even bite into one of New Mexico's famous chili peppers!

ancestors (AN-ses-terz) Relatives who lived long ago.

astronomy (uh-STRAH-nuh-mee) The science of the planets, moons, and stars.

civilization (sih-vih-lih-ZAY-shun) People living in a certain way.

climate (KLY-mit) The kind of weather a certain area has.

culture (KUL-chur) The beliefs, practices, and arts of a group of people.

electronic equipment (ih-lek-TRAH-nik uh-KWIP-ment) Tools used with computers and other high-tech gear.

enchantment (en-CHANT-ment) The condition of being very enjoyable or likeable.

nuclear (NOO-klee-ur) Having to do with the power created by splitting atoms, the smallest bits of matter.

observatory (ub-ZUR-vuh-tor-ee) A building in which scientists study the stars and the weather.

research laboratories (REE-serch LA-buh-ruh-tawr-eez) Places where scientists carefully study things and run tests.

ruins (ROO-enz) Old, falling-down buildings.

telescope (TEH-leh-skohp) An instrument used to study distant objects.

thrived (THRYVD) Were successful; did well.

weapons (WEH-punz) Objects or tools used to wound, disable, or kill.

New Mexico State Symbols

State Tree
Piñon Pine

State Animal
American Black
Bear

State Flag

State Bird
Greater
Roadrunner

State Flower
Yucca

State Seal

Famous People from New Mexico

Conrad Hilton
(1887–1979)
Born in Socorro
County, NM
Founded Hilton
Hotel Chain

William Hanna
(1910–2001)
Born in Melrose, NM
Animator

John Denver
(1943–1997)
Born in Roswell, NM
Singer and Songwriter

New Mexico State Map

Legend

○ Major City

✪ Capital

〜 River

New Mexico State Facts

Population: About 1,928,384

Area: 121,356 square miles (314,311 sq km)

Motto: "Crescit Eundo" (Grows as It Goes)

Song: "O Fair New Mexico," words and music by Elizabeth Garrett

Index

Web Sites

Due to the changing nature of Internet links, PowerKids Press has developed an online list of Web sites related to the subject of this book. This site is updated regularly. Please use this link to access the list:

www.powerkidslinks.com/amst/nm/